Songs
Faith
And
Feeling

www.davehopwood.com

The cover design is a photo of Scargill House, home to a fantastic Christian community, that welcomes guests for holidays, conferences and retreats, and is set in the Yorkshire Dales. A beautiful house and caring community and well worth a visit.

'Lives Shared, Lives Transformed.'

www.scargillmovement.org

A very big thanks to Martin Purnell for his proofreading and great encouragement.

And to all those who have given me such great feedback as these rewritten Psalms appeared on social media.

I'm no expert on the Psalms, no great theologian, I have just tried to bring my own understanding and worldview to these honest songs of prayer and praise. I love the reality in the Psalms, and the way that doubt, despair, anger, questioning, fear and frustration can be brought in a song of worship, as much as joy, peace, faith, adoration and praise. Years ago I heard someone ask the question – have we lost our nerve with God? And it's something I ponder on. Sometimes our praise is full of positive statements – nothing wrong with that – but life is full of all kinds of things, and we can surely bring all we are to God. We just sometimes seem to lack the worship songs to do this. That said, I am aware that more recently different lyrics are being written for worship.

If you have bought this on Kindle, firstly thank you, and I hope these writings are useful. Secondly, the paperback version of this has blank pages for your own comments, reactions, prayers and outbursts. You may like to keep a notebook nearby for your own thoughts as you make your way through this as an eBook.

I have not attempted all the Psalms, this collection originated as a series of daily thoughts posted on social media, so I may do more, but for now the list stands at 60. Originally I wrote these in a random order but for this book I have ordered them numerically. Four of them appear twice (!) – Psalms 27, 117, 139 and 145. Still, you can't have too much of a good Psalm.

I've not tried to reinterpret every line, but rather taken one or two themes that seem to leap out at me from each one and rethink these. Perhaps my thoughts will encourage you to record your own.

Towards the back you will find a few extras, prayers and readings which you may find useful for sharing or reflection. Please feel free to share any of this material with others if you think it will be helpful.

PS1

Like a tree planted in good ground,
Near a constant source of life and refreshment,
So that when the dry and trying times come,
It can still draw resources and vital nourishment.
Set our faces towards you, we pray.
Tune our minds and our wills and our hearts,
To your lifegiving song and resurrecting ways,
Draw us to that living water which not only gives us life,
But flows through us to those around,
Bringing light and strength to others,
Whether we are aware of this or not.

Psalm 1

PS2

So much turmoil and restlessness,
As the nations of the world toss and turn,
In the sleepless night of their searching,
In their attempts to assert themselves,
To make sense of their being,
To rule and reign and emerge as top dog.
Remind us again of your perspective
When we claim control and glory for ourselves.
Show us the better way,
Call us back to the crossroads of wisdom,
Guide us in the ancient paths of life,
As cherished children connected
To their loving Creator King,
Rather than rootless, lost things,
Meandering in random space and time.
Help us to wait, to serve, to hold on,
To plumb the depths of wisdom,
And to treasure once more the riches of grace,
Mined from the depths of your care for us.
And lead us once more to the security and joy
Of finding our place in you.

Psalm 2

PS3

Lord, for rest, for strength, for protection today,
For courage in the face of fear,
For justice and peace for so many,
Who face trouble and enemies today,
For faith in a world of misunderstanding,
For your presence when so many feel alone.
For light and truth and kindness,
And for the chance to play our part
In bringing these things to those we meet today.
For your name to be lifted up
And for your face to shine upon us.
For these and so many other things
We pray dear Lord, offering you
Our hopes, worries, anxieties and desires.

Psalm 3

PS6

You are the answer to our prayers,
You hear the cry of those lost,
Those longing for help and change,
Those whose tears are their constant friend,
Those in terror, those in torment.
The lonely hours give birth to these cries,
We can barely see straight at times,
But you understand all this,
You know the emptiness, the fear,
The desperation of a crucified life,
You know those times when grief and trouble
Rise like a tsunami, like waves threatening to engulf us.
We have faith, and we have fears,
We know trust, but we know trouble too,
Hear our cries for ourselves and others.
This world, our world, your world, longs for peace,
And so do we, may all that blots out the light
Be driven away, may truth and hope
Shine like the morning sun,
Warming our hearts and faces once more.

Psalm 6

PS7

We take refuge in you, our Lord,
We hide ourselves when the world
Seems bitter and overwhelming,
We press our faces to the rock that is higher than us,
Hold on to the one who is our salvation.
In this world of constant struggle
You are our shield, and our shelter,
You stand with us, before us and around us,
And how we need that.
How we need you to redirect the ways
Of a kingdom heading for destruction,
How we need your kindness and gentleness
When aggression and blame prevail.
May the powerful who lay traps,
Find themselves tangled in them,
May the weak find strength in you.
Help us to praise you once more,
And refocus our gaze on the desires of your heart.
For you made this world and its people,
You made us for life, care and justice,
Help us to want to want these things.

Psalm 7

PS8

Your presence etched in the stars,
A message twinkling in the night sky.
The Creator's handiwork,
Beyond the limits of my complex and troubled mind,
Larger than the margins of our understanding,
Yet available to the young,
To the curious and the small and humble,
With the perceptive simplicity of their thinking,
And the generous wonder of their worldview.
You set the wheels of time in motion,
You know each grain of sand,
And every curve and corner of the universe,
And yet you know us too, you know me,
And every curve and corner of our universes.
And though your creativity is vast,
So too is your love, your compassion,
Willing and ready to make your home in the centre
Of every human heart.

Psalm 8

PS13

To feel forgotten is a terrible thing,
To feel overlooked and pushed aside.
To want to slip away and curl up into a ball,
To think that no one see or cares,
This is a weight too great to carry.
But you see all things, and you understand,
You know the pains we carry, and the hurts,
You know the echoes from the past
That still ring in our ears.
You know the loss and disappointments,
The clouds that darken our nights and days.
Remind me of your kindness and help again today,
Turn your face to me once more,
And let your smile warm my heart please,
Rescue me and bring me to your place of peace.
Let a song rise within me to honour you,
Lift the burdens and scatter the darkness I pray,
And let your goodness bring love and healing.

Psalm 13

PS15

Without your invitation we can't draw close,
Without your kindness we can't get to know you.
Our lives are not blameless,
Our hands and hearts get sullied and muddied,
Truth is sometimes on our lips,
But so are gossip and rumour too.
We want to do good but at times do harm,
We want to be kind but sometimes are the opposite.
So we need your help, you've opened the door,
So that folks like me can draw near,
Can find forgiveness and daily new starts,
So we can know you and your ways a little more.
A new dawn each morning,
As the Son of righteousness rises once more,
Cleansing and refreshing and coaxing
Hope and kindness and trust within us.
Thank you.

Psalm 15

PS16

We come to you for all we need today.
Strengthen us we pray, keep us safe please,
Help us with the decisions we must make,
And show us the ways of life and kindness.
Though life is not straightforward or easy,
The good things we have come from you.
Remind us of those who have trusted you before,
Those heroes of love, hope and faith,
And help us to follow in their footsteps,
Though we are flawed and fragile at times.
Help us to make good choices, to lean towards the light,
For you are always with us, on our side,
Faithfulness is your watchword, and you have chosen
  us.
Help us to see again the wonder of knowing you,
Help us to find our place and peace in your hands,
Show us the way to life, the path of freedom,
And let the joy and comfort of your presence
Lift our hearts and give us purpose today.

Psalm 16

PS19

Some look at nature's masterpiece,
At the scribbling and the doodling of creation,
And see the signature of the creator,
God's autograph, writ large in the wild,
And the wonderful and the weird.
In the variety, the colours, the shapes and the shadows,
In the magnificence and the mystery of it all.
The endless extraordinaries you hold up your sleeve,
And produce in the colours and hues of our days and
  nights.
Can you have sleeves Lord... do you have them?
I'm going to trust and say 'yes' when considering your
  glory,
Your generosity, and the many ways you whisper,
Wave, sing, shout, pause and wait to grab our attention.
Calm us, slow us, help us to pause and wait,
So we don't miss those signs,
Those creation moments, those small glimpses of
  eternity,
Those precious clues, those treasured hints,
Enable us to take a breath every so often,
So the scales may drop from our eyes once more,
As we see again, as we sense you,
In the moments, in the wonder and the ordinary,
In the normal and unusual, in the dull and breath-
  taking.
Your fingerprints, your footprints, your smile
In the things you have made and given to us.
Psalm 19

PS20

May the Lord answer you in your troubles,
May he keep you safe and protect you,
May he give you strength and resilience,
May your worship delight and warm his heart.
May he grant you the desires of your heart,
And bless the hopes and plans you have.
May others be lifted by your dedication,
May they be helped, whether you know or not.
Some may look to earthly shows of power,
But we look beyond, to the compassion of God,
And to the strength and help that he can provide.
May we rise and stand firm in him,
May we sense his presence in the things of today.

Psalm 20

PS22

A cry of deep longing, of lament for others,
Of loud loss and lonely questioning,
Of disappointment too, and fear for ourselves.
Still full of faith... 'My God, my God...'
And within that faith finding room
For honest outpouring, and raw expression.
Having the nerve to trust that a faith
Beyond the shiny public sheen
Is a faith worth having, a true faith.
And a sadness too, remembrance of those gone before,
Of a glorious time when many had faith,
And we stand in their shadows, smaller somehow,
Or feeling that way anyway.
And a longing that our children might discover
The glorious faith that can cry out
In praise, trust, honesty and questioning,
Rediscovering their roots,
And the rock from which they were hewn.
Let there be a change, a new door opened,
A new relationship owned and celebrated,
And let us know you are with us,
When the sun shines and when the moon turns to blood.
Psalm 22

PS23

Lord, for ourselves, for those we care for,
And for those who lead us at all levels,
Please would you be our shepherd today.
Guiding us, providing what we need,
For the situations we all face.
When the going is rough may there be strength,
When the valleys are dark may there be light,
When our resources are low may there be
 replenishment,
When weariness takes hold may we find streams
Of refreshment, and calm inspiration.
When we are afraid may we sense you beside us.
Guide us we pray, lead us and help us,
And may we follow in your footprints today.
Amen.

Psalm 23

PS24

Far from random, no accident or evolutionary hiccup.
But a plan for meaning, a people known and designed.
Flawed yes, so flawed, but offered a rescue plan.
A daily beginning again, a regular place to drop burdens
And discover once more that we are highly valued.

This creation groaning, this universe wrestling with
 itself,
Once founded on sense and order,
Chaos calmed and light shattering darkness,
Breath on dust and something bursting from nothing.
A gift of stewardship, a place for creative nurturing.

And now the call goes out, whispered in the clouds,
Muttered in the regular and the irregular,
A rustling song in the cities and the small places,
The earth has a maker, who each day creates,
And we are his friends, his lovers and servants,
And Hope is our name, redemption in our DNA,
Flawed heroes, limping stars, supporting actors
In this great tale of daily struggle and opportunity.
Psalm 24

PS25

We offer you our hearts, minds, souls and strength,
Nurture trust in us please,
Lift us from distraction and despair,
Save us when the walls are closing in again.
There is a path, a way towards life and light,
And it is found in you.
Lead our steps please, our hurrying and dawdling,
Our resting, waiting and our busying,
Call to mind your unfailing compassion,
As you look down upon us,
Your inexhaustible kindness and love,
That well of goodness which never runs dry,
And forgive our mistakes and misdemeanours,
Our squabbling and sniping.
Help us to tune into your presence,
As we make our way through this day,
Drawing on your strength, courage, patience and
  gentleness,
So we may put our hope in you,
And your glory may shine through our flawed and
  fractured lives.

Psalm 25

PS27

Beneath everything, the bottom line,
The ground zero, the start and finish,
Before all, around and above,
To our left and right, on all sides,
You.
Our light, our life, in our waking and sleeping,
In our resting and working,
In our calling out and holding on,
In the restlessness for something more,
You.
Our place of safety and calm,
Our energy and courage to go on,
Our home and the path to life,
Our purpose, our reason and our rescuer,
You.
Help us to hold on, to wait for you,
To know you better, and to walk with you,
Shine your life on us, warm our hearts please,
Lift our heads and when the clouds gather,
Let the light of your presence break through once more.

Psalm 27

PS27

To be in your presence, and to know that
You are here, there and everywhere.
Your house being this present moment,
Your temple found in the workplaces,
The job centres, the sports grounds,
The shopping precincts, the leisure centres,
The library, the laundromats,
The queues and waiting places,
The supermarkets, our homes.
To know that we live with you and in you,
Through you and because of you.
Every breath, every move, every pause,
Our being found in your being,
Our light found in your light,
As you call us into relationship,
As you invite us to talk with you,
To bring our troubles and our fears,
The things we love and fear,
The things which hold us back,
And those things which move us on.
Be our source, our strength and our song today,
And hold us close to you, please.

Psalm 27

PS29

Imagine!! Mountains leaping madly like young calves,
Butting one another, skipping like lambs,
Hills twisting and turning and jiving and dancing,
Trying to outdo each other, to come up with the best
  moves,
Like lively children trying to be the king of the castle.
Deserts quaking, jumping out of their skin,
Rippling and tumbling like endless lines of dominoes.
Huge trees slapping a branch to their awesome trunks
Saying, 'Oh my goodness you made me jump!'
The whole of creation startled by the sound,
As the voice of reason, the voice of strength,
The voice of wonder and good humour,
Rattles around and makes everything sit up and take
  notice.
The voice of surprise and wisdom and laughter,
The voice that once whispered into the nothing,
And coaxed the first something into being.
The startling phenomenon of a God who laughs,
And smiles and enjoys what he has made,
Loves his people and draws close to us,
With peace and strength in his open hands.
Psalm 29

PS33

Let us honour the Lord,
Give him our time and energy,
Our plans and respect.
His perspective is so much greater than ours,
So much more detailed and understanding.
His view spanning the jigsaw of all time and every place.
In his hand he holds the keys of life and truth,
The keys of meaning, respect, dignity and justice.
So may we hold onto him and know that we are known.
May we find our joy and purpose in him,
The one who wired us up,
The one who put together the whole of the universe,
Every breath, every spark of life,
Every turning of the planets.
May we rediscover that gift of awe,
That blessing of knowing who we are in him.
Precious and created, not merely a cog in the machine,
But a vital part of his big picture.
May our hearts find wonder and confidence
In the one who is our maker and friend,
Our sword and shield and protector,
Our song of salvation and our way forward.

Psalm 33

PS37

The news can batter us
It can threaten our resolve,
Steal our hope and depress us.
The wicked seem to prosper and thrive,
The powerful weave destructive webs,
That ensnare and hurt those who are weaker.
Our songs, our cries, our prayers rise up for justice.
For peace and a better way.
And so... there is other news,
News that cuts against the grain,
A road less travelled, a different worldview,
One etched in the dust with the finger of God.
A call to trust in the one greater than our troubles,
To commit our worried and faltering steps to him,
To find wisdom in his ways,
To place our desires in him,
And to find peace and purpose in the one
Who invites us into his ever-expanding life.
To settle our hearts and minds on him,
And when they wander away, again and again,
To bring them back and settle them on him once more.
We have wisdom, we have love, we have kindness and
  strength,
But not enough, so let us bring our resources
To the one who is himself a well of life,
A living spring that never runs dry,
Rich in truth and love and goodness,
And on our side.
Psalm 37

PS39

There are times when I promise myself
I will behave better, and be a good person,
I set myself a standard and aim for it,
And before long find I am in the dust once more.
I try to be perfect, try to avoid the recurring mistakes,
But it just wears me out and leaves me disappointed.
The effort is too much, the bar is too high.
I forget what this thing is all about,
Forget about grace and mercy,
The grace of the gift of your presence each day,
The mercy of your forgiveness and help when I fall.
Forgive me for each day's pockets of rebellion,
And the wandering into selfishness and pride.
I am no superhero, though I would like to think I am,
But we *are* chosen and blessed and cherished,
Not merely shadows in your world, but guests,
Invited to be a part of your wonderful creation,
Not because we are great or strong or brilliant,
But because you are. Thank you.

Psalm 39

PS40

Help us to have patience, to wait for you,
To remember the times when you lifted us,
Show us again that you can make a way for us.
At times life feels like wading through mud,
The ground itself battles against us,
And the events of life push us back like a raging wind.
Help us to know you are thinking of us right now,
That your mind is set on us,
Lift us from the mire and the muddles that bring us
  down,
Strengthen us and help us not to be overwhelmed,
For you are our harbour, our source of help and
  nourishment.
Help us to look to you and to wait for you,
We do fear, but at times that fear will fade and
  dissipate,
Because you are with us, the king of justice and peace.
Your hands are strong enough to pull us from life's
  wreckage,
And your brightness shines strong in the darkness.
Rescue us, inspire us, sustain us, we pray.
Thank you.
Psalm 40

PS42

Like a car running low on fuel,
Or a battery drained of its power,
So we need you to keep going.
Our steps grow heavy,
Our purpose fades and falters,
We find ourselves searching for light,
In the shadows and the dull places.
We feel forsaken at times, forgotten and overlooked,
Our prayers expressed in our Gethsemane tears,
In cries and questions, that deep, deep longing.
We bring our restless hearts and eyes and minds,
These signs of our hopes and desires for more.
Our words dry up and we have only our silence,
And so we turn to you, you understand these things,
You know what it is to feel forsaken,
Let your kindness lift us up once more.

Psalm 42

PS46

God is with us, so we can bring our burdens to him,
He is on our side, an ever-present source of help.
Though it can often feel as if the whole world is
  shaking,
As if all we know is trembling beneath our feet,
As though life's rug is being pulled from beneath us,
Still our God is reliable and will not crumble or vanish.
He is a place of safety, we can hold onto him,
A house built on rock for the times when those storms
  come.
Calm yourself for a moment, he says in that still small
  voice,
Quieten yourself and draw close once more.
Find strength and wisdom and nourishment in me,
And know again that my love is for you,
And nothing can come between us,
Nothing at all can ever separate you from me.

Psalm 46

PS47

Some may be able to clap their hands,
For some it may be a clicking of fingers,
For others a clicking of their tongue,
A rolling of the eyes and a sigh.
But the call is there to come and offer something,
Anything really, I would say, a first step.
Hope imagines the rulers of the world,
Gathering in peace and worship,
A vision, a prayer for a better day.
For now we see the leaders at odds,
And worse, bickering, hostile, destructive,
The land is the Lord's, but we have snatched it,
Wrestled it from his grasp,
Like disgruntled tenants claiming it for their own,
Applying our own ideas of rule and reign,
And the poor suffer, the weak are trampled.
May we glimpse again the true glory of this world,
The rising of the king of justice and peace,
May we find our next step in him,
And may we not lose hope when things fall apart,
When the world seems as if it is lost in a dark room,
Blinkered, blundering and heading for a fall.
Lift us up Lord we pray, help us to bring our smiles,
Our mishaps, our longings, our regrets,
Our frowns, snarls, fears and dreams to you.
Psalm 47

PS51

How we need you Lord,
How we need you.
Your beauty, your strength, your clarity,
Each day threading through our lives.
For we fall and stumble,
Our strength fails and our vision dims,
Our clay feet grow heavy, and
We wander from the path of life.
Find ourselves wading through the mire
Of our bad choices and wilful ways.
Cleanse us and refresh we ask, please,
Restore our love and compassion,
Let the waterfalls of your grace
Wash us clean and revive us,
For without you we are weak and broken,
Without you we are lost and helpless.
Wake again the thirst for truth and hope,
Warm the embers of our longing for you.
Reset our coordinates,
So that we turn our faces once more,
To that which is full of life,
To that which can restore dignity and self-respect.
Thank you so much that you are gracious,
Slow to become angry and overflowing with love,
An ever-present help in the valleys of our troubles,
In the deserts of emptiness and times of our wanderings.
Help us to bring our broken spirits to you once more.

Psalm 51

PS57

May we take our confidence from you Lord,
May we find our strength and safety in you.
It is so easy to lose heart, to want to give up,
So easy to look to other things for comfort.
The world seems to open its jaws at times,
Roaring at us like a wild animal ready to pounce,
It seems fierce and ugly and raging and uncomfortable,
The walls close in and we feel surrounded.
Wake us up, stir us and take the scales from our eyes,
Help us to see you a little more clearly today,
To bring our fears and worries and doubts to you,
To find a source of strength in your faithfulness.
Be glorified Lord we pray, may your face shine like the
  sun,
And may your honour rise like the breaking dawn across
  our lands,
Shedding light and kindness and hope into our lives
  today.
Psalm 57

PS68

A good Father, a kind parent,
A carrier of burdens and worries,
One who lifts our heads and leads us,
The breaker of chains, and
In whose presence we find peace.
Glimpses of his wonder in the day's moments.
The one who cheers when we reach out,
When we show care and appreciation for others,
When someone lost is found,
When prisoners are freed, and lives rebuilt.
Break the power of the oppressors, we pray,
Those who glory in sneering and violence,
Those who line their pockets from others' misery.
Change this world so that truth is the song,
Gentleness the way of the strong,
And understanding is the universal language.
Change our world and change us,
Help us as we continue with those small things
That bring good change and share light.
May we sense the cheers of angels as goodness
Flies like a flag and kindness is the gift we bring.
Psalm 68

PS69

In the times when the floodwaters seem to rise,
When the view is littered with trouble,
When enemies of all kinds press in,
And the air crackles with the static of fear.
When the prejudiced appear to prosper,
And injustice lies like a feast for the cruel,
When we feel as if we are sinking in the mire,
And we are helpless to make a change...
We cry out to you, we pour out our troubles,
We stand in the gap for those who need you,
Those who face emptiness and catastrophe.
We bring our prayers and our pleas to you,
Our song of praise becoming a lament,
A cry for freedom, truth and change.
Turn the tables, transform the darkness please,
With the gentle and powerful light of your love.
Let the prisoners go free and the weak find strength,
Let life be restored in all its fullness,
May your unseen world of favour and kindness,
Break into our living once more and direct our ways,
And help us to keep on bringing our prayers to you.
Psalm 69

PS72

Give justice to our leaders, O God,
May it top their to-do list.
Help them judge and guide your people in the right way,
Let the poor always be treated fairly.
May the land yield peace and prosperity for all,
And may our lives be kind and fruitful,
Because fairness fills the land.
Help us to defend the poor,
To rescue the children of the needy,
And upend the plans of oppressors.
May your grace be as refreshing as the springtime rains
As it works its way through our lives.

Psalm 72

PS75

We praise you Lord at the start of this day,
And as the minutes and hours play out,
We take time to remember you.
This world is not as we would like it to be,
There is pain and loss and terrible injustice,
And at times peace on earth seems in short supply.
But we hold on to your promise that one day
Justice will prevail, truth and kindness will win,
And for now we will live in this land of waiting,
Where faith, hope and love matter so much.
And where weeds continue amongst the wheat.
We long for a better world, a different life,
We cry out to you for change and healing,
And in the meantime we celebrate the good things,
And cry out for help with all that needs change.
We proclaim your eternal affirming presence,
And look for the coming of your kingdom.

Psalm 75

PS84

Your home in us, and our home in you,
The longing of our heart, that restless call,
Finding its rest in you, in your house,
No longer made of stone but of flesh and blood,
Your presence finding its place in us,
Because of the endless possibilities of grace.
Our joy, our strength, our identity in you.
To be here, now, present with you,
Such a precious thing, worth everything,
Not running ahead of ourselves,
Or replaying the days of the past,
But centring ourselves in you, now,
The God of this moment, I Am,
May we be present as you are present.
With our tears, our frustrations, our questions,
Our smiles, our memories, our hopes,
We come with all of these and more,
For refreshment and protection,
For purpose and a way forward.
Oh Lord of all that is, you bring all you are to us,
Help us please to bring all we are to you.
Psalm 84

PS87

Home for all, a welcome for each of us,
From the four corners, and beyond,
Like a river streaming towards its source,
Like riders heading back through a storm,
So we find our place, our family.
Whatever background, experience, or life-story,
There is a home here for us,
A new life in this extraordinary community,
No longer exiles, drifters or rejected wanderers,
But citizens with passports that are eternal,
A people homeward bound, a land without fear,
A land without prejudice, blame or sorrow,
A place of fulfilment, innovation and safety.
Psalm 87

PS88

This song, this prayer, this cry of someone
Steeped in sorrow, buried in trouble,
Is one for all of us at times,
A sign that we may bring all we are,
No need for dressing up our lives in triumph,
Or photoshopping our faith when we come to God.
We can say it like it is, lay it all out,
Bring the complaints, the questions and the torrid
 anguish.
Feeling abandoned, cut off from care,
Hurled into the lowest, darkest kind of pit,
Unfairly treated and rejected, hurting and wounded,
And barely able to find words to express all this.
Bitten by life's vilest monsters,
Ambushed by catastrophe and malice.
On this day darkness is our one companion,
And out of that darkness we cry to our God,
Bringing every bit of our hearts and minds,
The loves, the loss, the cravings, the damage,
The bits of us we hide and the bits that are
 misunderstood.
All brought, all laid bare, in words and silence.
Expressed in the waiting and the tears,
And the longing for a burst of light and fresh air.
Psalm 88

PS93

The ocean roars and swells,
Rises and falls with its formidable surging,
The wind batters the coast with all its might.
The thunder crashes and bellows in the sky,
As if the clouds are in a shouting match,
The lightning cuts through the celestial canvas,
Jabbing its bright jagged way across the grey sky.
Hail batters on our doors and windows,
The knuckles of chilly weather grabbing our attention,
Rain dances rhythmically on our comings and goings,
Sapping strength and dousing our best laid plans.
But as powerful as these things are,
You are stronger, mightier, able to calm storms,
With your gentle power and stately strength.
Able to bring peace amidst the squalls and bluster,
That rage around us and within.

Psalm 93

PS103

You know our frailty, our temporary strength,
You know all about our ups and downs,
The dust and grit of our days and our nights,
You understand us better than we know ourselves.
Thank you for your grace and compassion,
Your kind and warm-hearted nature.
You take our blunders, foolishness, and fallouts,
Our mistakes and meandering and mess-ups,
And hurl them like a stone across the vast sea,
Disappearing into the mists of your forgiveness.
Your concern for us is endless,
Stretching forever, like the length of the horizon,
Immeasurable and inexhaustible.
Your glory rises like the colours of a new dawn,
It is wrapped in the shades of your love and integrity,
In the brilliance of your unfailing courage and
 tenderness.
Open our eyes once more to your ways,
Help us to cherish and respect you,
And to get to know you better, we pray,
Help us to draw daily on your strength and compassion.
Psalm 103

PS104

The bottom line, the ground zero,
The foundation to which we may return
When the world seems adrift,
And our ideas are shaken up once more.
You took dust and breath and imagining,
And made something new, something strong,
Winds roared and oceans came into being,
Planets came rushing at your calling,
And stars winked and twinkled at the sight.
Valleys and mountains took shape,
Land became fruitful and rippled with life,
Colours were born and light dawned and danced.
Plants and trees punched their way through the earth,
And crops spread like a carpet unravelling.
Creatures came yawning and sprawling,
Silent and small, crashing and colossal,
The universe crackled and fizzed with life,
As you broadcast your vision and things began.
Your glory whispers to us, seeping through all that is,
Your presence writ large in your creation
As it teems and trembles with life.
Your new start offers us a fresh beginning each day,
Each morning bringing life and forgiveness,
Purpose and hope, and the call
To be a vital and significant part
Of each day's ongoing creating.
Psalm 104

PS113

Praise the Lord,
In the quiet of a cool, breaking morning,
As the sun sends bright glimmers across the new day,
And in the reflective settling of evening,
As it sets in the curtain call of dusk.
In the quiet moments and the cluttered ones,
In silence and stillness and in gently muttered prayers,
In the songs of yesterday and today,
Let us offer the good moments and the struggles,
To one who refuses to stay distant, but reaches down,
Through the hands and help of those
Who care for the broken, and lift up the hurting,
Those who offer strength and comfort,
Those who stand for generosity and justice.
Let everyone everywhere, weak and strong,
Poor and rich, known and unknown,
From the far reaches of earth's four corners,
Offer their longings and their lives to you Lord.
Psalm 113

PS114

We read of your help in the past,
We hear of water gushing from dry rock,
Of the sea obeying your call and leaping out of the way,
A river changing its mind and taking a break from
  flowing,
Paths opening though the desert and a road in
  wilderness times.
We hear of mountains shivering at the sound of your
  voice,
Hills hearing their creator and craning their necks to
  look,
Of trees clapping their hands like excited toddlers.
The poetry of a people who know what rescue is,
The songs of liberation, wonder and desert dancing.
Put those same songs in our heart, we pray,
Make a path through our wildernesses,
Let the desert stream once more with fresh water,
And may the bright flowers of your salvation bloom,
And bring colour and meaning to our lives once more.
Strengthen us and help us to see the way, we pray,
Remind us of your presence with those words, 'Do not
  fear.'
Psalm 114 and Isaiah 35

PS117

We give you our praise,
As part of this precious, global family.
Help us to honour you in our jumbled lives,
Respect you as we live cradled in your world.
For you care for us with a love so deep,
A raging compassion which nothing can stop.
And though we may often lose our way,
Though we may stumble and fall,
Or forget about you, or disregard your presence,
You cannot forget us, you never disregard us,
Your face radiates kindness,
And your yearning for us burns ever brighter.
Psalm 117

PS117

The invitation to give honour to our Creator,
To recognise and praise him each day,
To respond to his presence revealed in the ordinary,
In the regular and the normal,
In the breath we take, and the steps we make.
The foot-washing servant, who designed a cosmos,
Invites us into each day's continued creating.
Not a distant deity but up-close and personal,
His care and kindness are faithful and true.
Though our fragile worlds tip and tumble,
His faithfulness is like a rock,
A sure anchor in the winds and the rains,
And in the turbulent mood swings
Of our ever-changing, restless universe.
His love goes on, reliable and robust,
So let us bring our praise, our faith and doubt,
Our feelings, gifts and questions,
Our wonder and our wondering,
And offer them as our worship.

Psalm 117

PS119

Your word is not always easy to understand,
Not the quickest of reads,
But your laws have life within them,
Your ways are saturated with energy.
The same verve that brought worlds into being,
And designed and created us, enveloped in these verses.
Sometimes the reading is like opening a window
And breathing in fresh air,
Sometimes it's like a long slow climb
Up a mountain to a whole new view.
Sometimes it's a rollercoaster,
And we feel exhilarated and upended,
Sometimes it's like a kaleidoscope,
And the colours and patterns make our eyes dance,
Sometimes the cover is like a lead weight,
Turning those pages is beyond our meagre strength.
Your word is not always easy to understand,
Not the quickest of reads,
But your laws have life within them,
Your ways are saturated with energy.
They are like a torch to light the path each day,
A support to steady our walking,
The deepest of breaths and a helping hand.
Open our minds to your treasures,
Warm our hearts with your wisdom,
Have patience as we question and wrestle,
And create in us a hunger for the words of life.
Draw us back to your precious, ancient crossroads,
So we may walk in the wise and lifegiving way.
Psalm 119, Isaiah 30 v 21, Jeremiah 6 v 16

PS120

Though this world may continue to burden us,
Though truth is trampled at times,
And peace crumpled and thrown aside,
We have somewhere to bring our fears,
Somewhere to offload the weight of sorrow.
At times we may feel far from home,
In a land of sorrow, misdirection and spite,
Yet your light shines on in the darkness,
In the eyes and lives of those who love peace,
Those who hold on to compassion and truth.
The way at times feels narrow and uneven,
The walls close in and we are sore from walking,
Even so call us on, and remind us that you understand,
You are truth and life, peace and hope,
And we can bring our fears and pain to you,
Each day, each night, each moment, each step.
Psalm 120

PS121

We lift our eyes up
To that which is higher,
To that which is greater,
Calmer, more patient, more robust,
Than we are.
We lift our eyes up,
And remind ourselves,
Of your creativity,
Which continues in our lives,
Your strength, your care for us.
We lift our eyes up,
To the one who doesn't tire as we do,
Doesn't grow weary or get stressed.
See us through this day, we pray,
Help us as we go, please,
As we climb these mountains,
And when the going is easier.
And help us to keep on,
Lifting our eyes, lifting our gaze,
To you from time to time.

Psalm 121

PS123

At times we may feel self-reliant,
Strong enough, wise enough, on our own,
But then our eyes are opened once more,
And we realise yet again how much we need you.
And so we look to you now Lord,
Like a new child looks up wide-eyed,
Held in its mother's protective arms,
Unable to do anything to earn that love and care.
So we lift our eyes and our needs to you now.
As a lost traveller needs their compass,
As walkers look to their guidebooks and maps,
We look to you for mercy, kindness and strength,
Aware that this world is limited, and you are not.
Fill us again with your spirit of knowledge and truth,
Of reality, confidence, depth and reverence,
And keep nudging us to look to you.

Psalm 123

PS127

We each have our skill set and our abilities,
Our passions, hobbies and likes,
And the best thing we can do as we use them,
Is to commit our ways to the Lord,
To offer all we can and are to him.
We can do much in our own strength
And with our own understanding,
And bringing all we do and plan to him,
Is like bringing the seeds we sow to be watered.
We can only do so much ourselves,
But God's strength and understanding go further,
His resources are generous and endless,
And he is the one who brings lasting fruit
From the things we do, our work, rest and
 commitments.
With him we can do more than we expected,
In him we find the source and spring of all life.
Psalm 127

PS130

Like waiting for the light of a new dawn,
As it edges over the horizon,
We wait for you, wait for your help.
Hurry on please, don't delay.
Your forgiveness is like the best nutritious food,
Like a daubed wall wiped as clean as new,
Like the fragrance of fresh flowers,
Bringing peace and a smile.
You bring rescue like no one else can,
Your inclination is always towards us.
You choose love over anger,
Forgiveness instead of blame,
And so your words lift us up,
Rather than destroying us,
They make life better, not worse.
Your road rises to meet us,
And you give us the strength to travel.

Psalm 130

PS131

Lord rein in my thoughts please,
(And reign in them too!)
When they run away with themselves.
When I think too much of myself,
When I set myself on a flimsy, cobweb pedestal,
All too easily brought crashing down in the next breath.
But save me too when my thoughts turn to worry,
When I catastrophise and imagine the worst,
When my head becomes a battleground of fear,
When anxiety blocks out light and hope.
Help me to bring these things to you,
Turn them into an honest burst of worship.
Teach me again to trust and rest,
As a tiny child trusts and rests,
And looks to the one who carries it.
Psalm 131

PS133

To work for peace, to pray for it,
To long for it and search for it,
To give ourselves to that way of life,
Is a precious and vital thing, and the call of heaven.
It is nourishment and refreshment,
Blessing and encouragement for others,
It's a precious and incomparable offering,
An act of respect and worship,
That brings warmth to the heart of God.
It makes life better rather than worse,
It is sweet rain on the deserts of our lives,
Causing forgotten flowers to grow again,
It brings colour and light and strength.
It's like a cool drink on a blistering day,
A welcome instead of expected rejection.
The way of harmony, of unity and peace,
Is no easy calling, not trouble-free, or straightforward,
But worth it. And heaven rings with applause.
Psalm 133

PS134

The invitation to bless you Lord,
The one who invented blessing,
That we might, with our dusty hands,
And muddled, sweat-stained lives,
Give you honour and respect.
Though we have feet of clay
And our minds are often chaotic and cluttered,
Yet we can be part of glorifying you,
Praising your name wherever we are,
In the temple of our everyday lives.
Psalm 134

PS135

Though today's roads may wind and weave uphill,
It is good to remember when the way was smooth,
When the going was easier.
Though the horizon is currently grey,
It is helpful to recall the days of sun,
The times when grace was with us,
When purpose and kindness were like energy
That got us leaping out of bed each day.
When the gusts of vision and meaning
Were like divine breath in our sails,
Moving us on, helping us sail through the storms.
Though our understanding is muted and limited,
Save us from diving down into despair,
Rescue us from the potholes that bring us down,
The traps that trip us and make us tumble.
Bring our focus back on you, clear our gaze please,
And lift the scales so we can see the way once more.
Save us we pray, from trusting in those things
Which merely make the going harder,
Set us free from holding on to the distractions,
If they only add to the mist and the haze.
Let your Son break through and guide our step today,
Even if we find it hard to tune in,
Hard to know that you are with us.
Guide us and lead us, and let there be moments
When grace and peace lift our spirits once more.
Psalm 135

PS136

We are born. We cry. We fill nappies and drink milk.
His love, his kindness, his caring presence is always with us.
We grow. We struggle. We learn. We tumble.
His love, his kindness, his caring presence is always with us.
We throw food. And tantrums. And opinions. And plans.
We get hormones. And shape. And strength. And ideas.
His love, his kindness, his caring presence is always with us.
We work. We skive. We play. We sleep. We think. We do.
We hurt. We lose things. We wonder what happened. We break.
His love, his kindness, his caring presence is always with us.
We question. We shout. We laugh. We mutter. We whisper.
We wonder if we are normal, we try to fit in, we have good days and bad.
His love, his kindness, his caring presence is always with us.
We lose games. We lose people. We lose our way. We lose in life.
We have good times. We have bad. We have both together.
We are quiet. We are noisy. We long for friends. We want to be alone.
We worship, we sing, we pray, we cry out, we rant, we smile, we frown.
His love, his kindness, his caring presence is always with us.
We discover God's love, we lose sight of it again.
We feel God loves us, then we don't, then we hope he does.

We hold onto our Creator, we have nowhere else, no one
  like him.
We push him away, we run back, we escape, we limp
  home.
*His love, his kindness, his caring presence is always with
  us.*
We don't understand him, we wish we did.
We keep on, walking, wheeling, limping, running,
  shuffling.
We love him, and our love is often small, big, weak,
  empty, guarded,
full, dedicated, compromised, strong, distracted,
  embarrassing, limited,
powerful, shallow, exuberant, lacking, unique, unusual,
  precious.
*His love, his kindness, his caring presence is always with
  us.*
Psalm 136

PS137

At times we find ourselves adrift,
Our reference points have shifted
And we are not sure how to find you.
It seems too hard, too strange here,
As we search for signs of your presence.
Help us to break through the unfamiliar,
The sense that all is lost.
Calm our fears, our anger and frustration,
Comfort us in our trouble and loss.
Let us know you are right here with us,
That we are not abandoned,
Give us the words to pray once more,
To reach beyond ourselves,
And reconnect with the one who knows
All places, all experiences, every inch of life,
Every step we take, and every moment
When we feel grounded, unsure and afraid.
Psalm 137

PS139

To be known by you
And to know you with us
In all we do, wherever we go.
In the waking and living,
In the stumbling and bleary-eyed mornings,
In the pressure to get things done,
In the pauses for coffee, tea and thought,
In the waiting and getting things done,
In the failing and achieving,
As we soar on wings like eagles,
And as we trip over our own feet.
In the light and the dark,
In the moments of confusion and understanding.
In our praying and distractions,
In our arguments and disappointments,
In the tough moments and the nothing times,
In the wonder and the unexpected laughter.
Known by you, knowing you with us,
No part of our day or night beyond
Your kind and strong and understanding reach.
Psalm 139

PS139

I could ask the darkness to hide me,
Run into the night, slide under a blanket,
And you would be there, always there,
Even in darkness I cannot hide from you,
You have been there, knowing loneliness and fear,
You have experienced the worst of things,
You're unafraid of the darkness around and within.
To you there is always light,
And the darkness cannot extinguish it,
Like a candle we blow out that reignites,
The light goes on because you go on,
For you are the light, and indestructibly so.
And though we once tried to extinguish you,
It gave you the chance to plunge into the depths,
Travel to the darkest corners and grimmest pits,
And re-emerge with the light of a new dawn.
The Son rising, the light forever returned.
Hope sealed with a resurrection promise.
And so the night shines as bright as day to you,
And though darkness may often present itself,
At times seeming like our only friend,
Darkness and light are both alike to you,
And so we cry out once more,
Let your light shine and may the darkness flee.
Psalm 139 v 11-12

PS143

When we feel broken down,
When the world won't go our way,
We have somewhere to bring our troubles,
Our weariness and disappointment.
When we feel as if the walls are closing in,
And hope just left through the back door,
When fear threatens to hold us prisoner,
We have somewhere to bring these things,
A place where we can pour out our angst,
And offload the burdens we so often carry.
Remind us of your great love,
Of your presence and gentle understanding.
Help us to rediscover our vision of you,
Your majesty and soaring greatness,
And your ability to set our feet on rock.
Save us from these things which bring us down,
Rescue us and show us again your wonder.
Help us to take another step,
And to worship and serve you once more,
For without you we often stumble and wander,
With you so much is possible.
Thank you that you are on our side,
Closer than the air around, a guide
In the storms and our energy when we fall.
Psalm 143

PS145

So much of life fills my head,
So many images and thoughts collide,
Squashed in like too many people in a lift,
Too much furniture in a small space.
Refresh my mind O Lord,
Bring it back to focus on you,
To bless you and praise you once more,
Though my words may be small
And my song a little on the quiet side.
Your compassion falls like rain on the hills,
Your gracious welcome wraps around us,
Like the warmth of the sun on the first spring day,
You are faithful and dedicated to us,
Even when our faithfulness dries up.
Lift us when we fall, please,
Support us with the burdens we carry,
Help us to walk and not grow weary,
Keep us hungry for more of you,
And let the desires of our heart find their place in you.
And as we look to you may others follow our gaze,
And discover you too, with us each day,
As we find our place in you,
May that help others to do the same please.
For you are mighty and magnificent,
Gentle and tender, eternal and this present moment,
Help us to celebrate you in our silence,
In our songs and our bumbling lives,
And be our rest in the clutter of our days.
Psalm 145

PS145

I don't always feel this way Lord,
But there are times when praise bubbles up,
Gratitude, respect, and worship overspill
In a song scribbled from my heart.
Improvised and full of gladness and glory,
My gladness and your glory,
Like a poet grabbing a pen and an old scrap of paper,
And inscribing for all their worth,
Because they cannot contain the words,
Can't hold back the expression exploding within them,
Like a verbal volcano of untidy adulation.
The wonders of you captured in a cry,
Your gracious kindness etched on a flesh'n'blood
  napkin,
In a string of verbs and nouns and adjectives.
A glimpse of your spectacular nature,
Your greatness and compassion and splendour,
Clumsily captured in a few crafted phrases,
Not word perfect, but that's not the point,
The point is you, and who you are,
And for a few moments I forget myself,
And the complaints I harbour,
And the dissatisfaction with life,
And I remember and celebrate you,
And in doing so I am for a while, lifted.
Psalm 145

PS146

I give myself a reminder, a nudge,
To remember to say thank you,
To remember to bring my praise to God.
Remembering the one who sets captives free,
Who opens prison doors, and lets the light in,
The one who opens our eyes to grace and truth.
The one who does not lay heavy burdens on us,
But lifts up those who struggle to keep going,
The one who will not break a bruised reed,
Or put pressure on those already weighed down.
The one who leans towards the rejected and hurting,
The one who turns us towards those who need help.
The one who loves it when we offer kindness,
The one who is glorified when we care.
The true king, reigning long after leaders rise and fall,
The creative commander of compassion,
For all time, for all nations, for all generations.
Psalm 146

PS150

Praise the Lord!
Praise him with all we are,
And all we can do.
Whatever our strengths and weaknesses,
Whatever our gifts and abilities.
Sport, music, baking, cooking,
Sewing, knitting, speaking, listening,
Fixing things, making stuff,
Science and problem solving,
Planting and growing,
Researching and calculating.
Quietly or with sound or music,
Alone and with others,
In private and public,
Devoted and distracted,
Not worrying about the right words.
Let everything that has breath,
Take some moments to focus
On our creator and say:
Thank you, and bless you,
And we love, respect and honour you.
Psalm 150

A FEW EXTRAS

Each Wednesday I post up what I call *Lyrical Riffs* on social media, in some ways my own kind of psalms. I thought I'd include them here in case any are useful.

Song

Lord, we offer you the psalm of our life,
The song of our being and doing,
With its tuneful notes and its discordant ones,
The peaceful parts and the clattering.
The rousing chorus of the celebratory times,
And the sorrowful verses that rise from the worry
And the times of trouble and fear.
Thank you that you are in all the notes,
All the beats and pauses of my life.
You know the songs of our waking and sleeping,
The parts so quiet we can barely whisper them,
The parts so painful the tune is held inside us.
The songs of finding and losing,
The songs of holding and letting go,
Songs of moving forward and songs of being stuck,
Songs of achieving and failing, doing and not doing,
The notes rise and fall, and fade and sound again.
You know them all, and share in these tunes,
Bringing your own song of understanding.

A Prayer for Peace

Lord we pray today for peace in your world,
For those working to bring peace,
For those longing to live in peace,
For those with the power to offer peace.
Lord for the vulnerable and the young,
For the oppressed and the frightened,
For those who feel forgotten and trapped.
We pray for them and for ourselves.
Blessed are the peacemakers, you said,
We pray for blessing on them and on their work,
On those labouring tirelessly to bring peace and safety,
And for the powerful and the strong
That they might bring hope and freedom and kindness.
Lead us, guide us, urge us and inspire us we pray,
Make us all peacemakers in the small and significant
  things,
May we be part of your big picture of hope
And kindness in this world today we pray,
Keep us going, keep us praying, keep us open and
  hoping,
And keep us following your way of peace please,
Amen.

Gratitude

If you had not entrusted yourself to us,
Where would we be, I wonder.
If you had not entrusted yourself
To that young poor couple in Bethlehem,
If you had not chosen to walk those streets
Of oppression, loneliness, fear and hardship,
If you had not chosen the way of service
Of washing feet, healing hearts and sacrifice,
Where would we be, I wonder.
If you had not set aside the glories of heaven,
And chosen to walk the gutters and side streets,
The wide roads and narrow alleys of this world,
If you had not set aside the glories of heaven,
And chosen to walk the gutters and side streets,
The wide roads and narrow alleys
Of my heart and mind and soul and will,
If you had not entrusted yourself to us,
With understanding and compassion in both hands,
Then where would we be, I wonder?
Where would I be? Thank you.

I Still Believe

I still believe, though I'm often haunted by doubt,
I still believe, though the road goes uphill at times.
I still believe in truth though life has its shams,
I still believe in safe-distancing though I often forget,
I still believe in caring though I often don't.
I still believe in trying, though I often fail,
I still believe in the light though the clouds hover,
I still believe in hope, in spite of the despair.
I still believe in grace, though blame hangs heavy,
I still believe in You, and believe You believe in me,
Though the questions and distractions mount up.
I still believe in changing the world one smile at a time,
And I still believe that we were made for love and peace.
And I still believe we are no accident, all precious and
  unique,
And I still believe that You are the source of all hope and
  life.
I still believe.

Pruning

I am the true vine, and my father is the gardener.
He prunes every branch in me that bears fruit.
Lord, that's easy to read, trips off the tongue,
But who wants to be pruned? I mean... *really*?
I came for all the benefits, all the upwardly-mobile stuff,
All the good and refreshing and happy things.
I didn't come to be changed, to be transformed,
I mean... I might not cope, it all feels like hard work.
Someone once said that you accept us just as we are,
And I believe that, I need that, I hold onto that.
It's a precious thing in a harsh world of judgement.
But they also said that you love us too much
To leave us as you find us. You want to bring more from
us,
To make more possible for us. To bring fullness and life.
And that requires change and development.
Like a garden being primed for fruit,
Rather than left free for the incursion of weeds.
Ho hum. Oh dear. Help! I can't do this alone.
Thank you that you also said, 'Come to me if you are
wrecked,
If you are shattered, exhausted, broken from this life.
For my ways are good and my patterns are better.'
And so, in my wrestling I hold onto both,
The pruning and the uplift, the change and the
acceptance.
Thank you that you promised not to break a bruised
reed,
Or put out those of us who are small, flickering lights.
Thank you.

Two Prayers

In the Garden of Gethsemane
Jesus prayed two prayers:
'Rescue me' and 'Let it be.'
'If possible take this cup from me.'
Then, 'Not my will but yours.'
Two prayers often on our lips.
Though it is often hard to know
Which is the right one,
And we hover between both prayers.
'Rescue me, set me free from this.'
Or 'Let it be, your will be done in and through me.'
Either way be glorified in us please,
Though we often feel anything but glorious.
Let your will be done, let your glory shine
Through the gaps and cracks and flaws,
And if we take wrong turns,
Then take those too and shine through please,
It's hard to pray 'Let it be' at times,
Sometimes it's hard to even utter, 'Rescue me.'
Be our strength, be our prayer today please.

On Prayers and Praying

What of our prayers and praying?
They are like a hand reaching for help and comfort
And something solid for ourselves and others,
A song we make up as we go along,
Expressing our sometimes honest,
Sometimes rehearsed pleas and praise.
A way of drawing near to one who knows us,
A way of standing with the one who gave all
On that lonely Gethsemane night,
Waiting with him, like waiting with a child
Who fears the dark and asks for our company.
A means of discovering more than we can know
Merely by our own efforts and means,
A way of discovering the nature and character
Of the one who created our nature and character.
A light in the dark, a calming voice in the night,
A way home, a path to redemption,
A friend in the chaos and the muddle,
A way of finding forgiveness, and forgiving
Ourselves and one another.
An anchor in the inevitable storms,
A refuge when life's weathers batter us once more.
A smile when we feel surrounded by scowls.
A way of absorbing divine kindness and generosity.

A New Day

For hope, for comfort, for strength,
For signs of another life, a new day.
For laughter after the tears,
For sunshine after the rain,
For healing after the heartache,
For rebuilding after the destruction,
Hope after the despair,
Peace after the chaos,
Moving on after hitting the wall,
Change after the stagnation,
Communication after the silence.
For songs of friendship after the sniping,
For celebration after the lamenting.
For repair after the ruin,
For getting up after the falling,
For strength after the shattering,
And kindness after the complaining,
For welcome after the blaming,
For reality after the fakery,
For warmth after the cynicism,
For love after the loss.

Revelation 21 v 5, Isaiah 43 v 19

All

To offer it all, our whole being, the bits we like and the
  bits we don't.
Like Jacob wrestling with an angel, we wrestle in our
  love for God,
We wrestle with our dedication,
Our longings, our mistakes and missteps,
Our hearts like a colour-by-numbers chessboard,
Bits that are impressive and brightly shaded,
Bits that are less so, and patchy and grey,
Bits that are downright darkly splodged, hardly a work
  of art at all.
And so we hide behind our rocks, behind our masks and
  fig leaves,
While the call comes to us,
'Let me see you, bring all you are, let me hear you and
  receive you.'
The invitation to offer all of our all,
Hearts, minds, souls, strength, our stumbling and
  jumbled thinking.
Not in perfect condition, far from it,
But because there is One who gets us,
Understands and cherishes the children he made.
To offer it all, our whole being,
Not because our love is strong and unfailing,
But because His love is, his kindness reliable,
His love beyond all we can grasp, strong and smiling,
An open door, a welcome mat, a warm embrace.
Like a father hurtling at breakneck speed to
Welcome home his lost and hurting children,
With all our grief, disappointment, and frustration,
His heart pounding and poured out for us.

Open Hands

To live a life with open hands,
I think must be a wonderful thing,
Risky, and vulnerable, of course
Yet also free of the compulsion to hold onto things,
Free of the stress of needing to control.
The freedom of the open life,
Turns the days into a flesh and blood poem,
Albeit a random and meandering one,
Where the unexpected is warmly embraced,
And strangers are seen as friends.
To live a life with open hands,
Must be a costly thing,
Threatening to some for whom freedom
Is a dangerous principle,
And before too long, hands so open
May well be pierced and pinned up.
But the freedom of such an open life
Cannot perhaps be so restrained,
And while such hands might hold
Compassion, sacrifice, struggle and pain,
There is also room in there for resurrection,
And the rising sun on an open-tomb morning.
To live a life with open hands
Now that's something I cannot do,
But I know someone who lived that way,
And continues to do so.

Fuel

It matters
What we put in,
What we take on board,
What we absorb and hold on to.
Or to put it another way,
The saying goes:
Feed the healthy person within.
Though that's not always easy.
Sometimes we cannot help the
Graffiti sprayed on the depths
Of our being by others.
So we need new messages,
Words of hope, words of life,
Words that pat us on the back,
Rather than stabbing us.
Messages with meaning and
Identity, rather than labels.
Roadmaps that lift us and take us on,
Leading us back together,
Rather than lonely dead-ends.
Give hopelessness a wide berth, hug mercy,
Top your to-do list with kindness,
Absorb the kind of truth that sets us free.

Fretting

We fret about so many things
Surviving, success, stability,
Being accepted, being strong,
Our looks, our finances, our family.
Those we love, those we like, those we fear,
Our past, our present, our future.
How we will make it through the days,
The nights, and the months to come.
There is a song beyond the white noise of worry.
A tune that calls us to lift our eyes,
Above the onslaught of discordant days,
To one who offers friendship, wisdom, and trust.
Confidence for the steps we must take,
Not demanding we become something else,
But drawing us closer to him,
So he may draw true humanity from us,
Calming the panic that rages,
And the nagging pressures which wear us out.
An understanding guide, a source of strength,
For the fretting and the white noise.
So many things call for our attention,
But one thing can change our perspective.

Luke 10 v 38-42

If

If you are the Way, the winding path,
Then surely nobody knows how to get home
Without you.
If you are the Life, the source,
Then perhaps nobody breathes or moves
Without you.
If you are the Truth, the reality,
Then anything we see clearly,
Any vital discoveries,
Any good and precious knowledge,
Come from you.
If we live and move and have
Our being in you,
If nothing that is was made without you,
If you are the Alpha and Omega,
The beginning, end and middle
Of all of life's endeavours,
Then to know you is beyond precious.
Beyond wisdom and all our good ideas,
It is life, truth and love itself.
In you we find ourselves,
Our true north, and our home forever.

For Us

For the fathers, the fathered, and the fatherless,
For the mothers, the mothered, and the motherless,
For the mentors and the role models,
For the carers and those they care for,
For the children, the young, and the young at heart,
For the peaceful and the troubled,
For those embracing responsibility,
And for those overwhelmed by it,
For the hopeful and the anxious,
For those who bring joy and those who need it,
For you and me, for this moment, this day:
See how much our Heavenly Father loves us,
He cares for us so much he has made us
His children.

Calling

Lord we long for you,
As dry ground longs for rain,
As sports fans long for a win,
As weary travellers long for rest.
Lord we thirst for you,
Our parched souls calling out,
With words we can barely express,
In our fears for the future,
And our hopes for something more.
Lord how we need you,
As a body needs breath,
As people need vision,
As lives need bread and water.
Lord we long for you,
Each day, each hour, each moment,
Sustain us, inspire us, transform and help us,
For our hope, our peace, and our glory
Are in you.
Amen.

Salvation

A many layered gift,
Moving us from darkness to light,
From fear to compassion,
From rejection to welcome,
From lost to found,
(Though we may struggle to find ourselves at times)
From one worldview to another.
Getting us through the day,
Through the next hour,
Over this hurdle, up that mountain,
Past those molehills,
Lighting up the next footstep.
Offering us direction and purpose,
Another dimension to this life,
Eyes, ears, hearts... doors opened,
A life of days endless, a promise of more to come.
A living letter, a message of being cherished,
Valued, understood, called and precious.
A changing thing, a road to walk,
Gentle and profound, powerful and simple,
Summed up in two words: 'Follow me.'
A daily new start from that man from Galilee.

Ordinary

You take what is ordinary,
And make it extraordinary.
You take what is overlooked,
And make it significant.
You took one small boy's lunch,
And made it into a feast,
You took six jars of water,
And made a celebration,
You took a cross of despair,
And made it into an eternal sign of hope.
You take our fragmented lives,
And shine out through the gaps,
You take a little love and a little faith,
And use it to change the world.
You take what is ordinary,
And make it extraordinary.

Twilight and Dusk

Lord help me to find You and know You,
Through the changes in this shifting world.
You see, things falter, I get confused,
The mist comes down, the landmarks shift,
And the goalposts are all out of line.
Help me believe again, to reach for You again,
And to believe that You hear this cry,
And to believe that You can do something,
That these words matter to You.
Help me when the prayers, the desire,
The trust... have been replaced with questions,
And what used to be, is now something else.
I'm out of ideas here,
Caught between twilight and dusk,
Soft light and shade.
Some of us here seem strong and sure,
Some of us less so,
Yet we are all part of this one diverse body.
Help us to find You,
Our realistic, irreligious, experienced Creator,
And help us please, to be found by You.

Printed in Great Britain
by Amazon